Questions lovingly answered by:

How do I love thee? Let me count the ways.
I love thee to the depth and breadth and height
My soul can reach, when feeling out of sight
For the ends of being and ideal grace.
I love thee to the level of every day's
Most quiet need, by sun and candle-light.
I love thee freely, as men strive for right.
I love thee purely, as they turn from praise.
I love thee with the passion put to use
In my old griefs, and with my childhood's faith.
I love thee with a love I seemed to lose
With my lost saints. I love thee with the breath,
Smiles, tears, of all my life; and, if God choose,
I shall but love thee better after death.

— Elizabeth Barrett Browning —

What is the best gift you've ever given someone? Why did you give them that gift?

☐ HER REPLY ☐ HIS REPLY

☐ HIS REPLY ☐ HER REPLY

How strong you think you are?

☐ HER REPLY ☐ HIS REPLY

☐ HIS REPLY ☐ HER REPLY

When was the last big thing you played and how'd you feel playing it?

☐ HER REPLY ☐ HIS REPLY

☐ HIS REPLY ☐ HER REPLY

How do you deal with your inner child?

☐ HER REPLY ☐ HIS REPLY

☐ HIS REPLY ☐ HER REPLY

What should you not do at night, if you're not going to sleep?

☐ HER REPLY ☐ HIS REPLY

☐ HIS REPLY ☐ HER REPLY

Why do you have to be the hero of your world?

☐ HER REPLY ☐ HIS REPLY

☐ HIS REPLY ☐ HER REPLY

Do you think your life is easy? Why or why not?

☐ HER REPLY   ☐ HIS REPLY

____

____

____

____

____

____

☐ HIS REPLY   ☐ HER REPLY

____

____

____

____

____

____

Would you rather take this deal? Why?

☐ HER REPLY   ☐ HIS REPLY

____

____

____

____

☐ HIS REPLY   ☐ HER REPLY

____

____

____

____

Do you have a secret that no one can know about you? Why?

☐ HER REPLY   ☐ HIS REPLY   ☐ HIS REPLY   ☐ HER REPLY

If you could have any of the world's finest musicians play for you, what music would they play?

☐ HER REPLY   ☐ HIS REPLY   ☐ HIS REPLY   ☐ HER REPLY

Which decade of clothing fashion was your favorite and least favorite?

☐ HER REPLY ☐ HIS REPLY

☐ HIS REPLY ☐ HER REPLY

If you could only take one item out of this book, what would it be?

☐ HER REPLY ☐ HIS REPLY

☐ HIS REPLY ☐ HER REPLY

Given the chance to give your child only one quality as a person, which would you choose?

☐ HER REPLY ☐ HIS REPLY

☐ HIS REPLY ☐ HER REPLY

Say something about your character that annoys you

☐ HER REPLY ☐ HIS REPLY

☐ HIS REPLY ☐ HER REPLY

Would you rather have the ability to create a new set of memories at will or not?

☐ HER REPLY ☐ HIS REPLY   ☐ HIS REPLY ☐ HER REPLY

_______________________________   _______________________________
_______________________________   _______________________________
_______________________________   _______________________________
_______________________________   _______________________________
_______________________________   _______________________________
_______________________________   _______________________________
_______________________________   _______________________________
_______________________________   _______________________________
_______________________________   _______________________________

List of things that makes one smile

☐ HER REPLY ☐ HIS REPLY   ☐ HIS REPLY ☐ HER REPLY

_______________________________   _______________________________
_______________________________   _______________________________
_______________________________   _______________________________
_______________________________   _______________________________
_______________________________   _______________________________
_______________________________   _______________________________
_______________________________   _______________________________

Why should you watch that show?

☐ HER REPLY ☐ HIS REPLY

☐ HIS REPLY ☐ HER REPLY

Describe a time when you realized you were behaving like your mother or father and how that experience helped you better understand your parent.

☐ HER REPLY ☐ HIS REPLY

☐ HIS REPLY ☐ HER REPLY

What is something that has been a huge source of pain or disappointment for you?

☐ HER REPLY ☐ HIS REPLY   ☐ HIS REPLY ☐ HER REPLY

What makes people fall out of love with you?

☐ HER REPLY ☐ HIS REPLY   ☐ HIS REPLY ☐ HER REPLY

How would you describe the feeling of being haunted?

☐ HER REPLY   ☐ HIS REPLY

____
____
____
____
____
____
____

☐ HIS REPLY   ☐ HER REPLY

____
____
____
____
____
____
____

How would you describe the feeling of being like one with the heavens?

☐ HER REPLY   ☐ HIS REPLY

____
____
____
____
____

☐ HIS REPLY   ☐ HER REPLY

____
____
____
____
____

How do you want to be known?

☐ HER REPLY ☐ HIS REPLY

☐ HIS REPLY ☐ HER REPLY

Do you believe that you have to utter a wish every 11:11 PM? Why?

☐ HER REPLY ☐ HIS REPLY

☐ HIS REPLY ☐ HER REPLY

Say something about yourself that's different from the norm

☐ HER REPLY ☐ HIS REPLY

☐ HIS REPLY ☐ HER REPLY

What's something your brain tries to make you do and you have to will yourself not to do it?

☐ HER REPLY ☐ HIS REPLY

☐ HIS REPLY ☐ HER REPLY

What's the worst that could be?

☐ HER REPLY ☐ HIS REPLY

☐ HIS REPLY ☐ HER REPLY

How do you deal with the negative effects?

☐ HER REPLY ☐ HIS REPLY

☐ HIS REPLY ☐ HER REPLY

Tell me about one of your earliest memories. Write down anything you can remember.

☐ HER REPLY ☐ HIS REPLY   ☐ HIS REPLY ☐ HER REPLY

What are the three things you want to do this summer?

☐ HER REPLY ☐ HIS REPLY   ☐ HIS REPLY ☐ HER REPLY

Say something about your ear shapes

☐ HER REPLY ☐ HIS REPLY

☐ HIS REPLY ☐ HER REPLY

If you could choose what to come back as, what would it be?

☐ HER REPLY ☐ HIS REPLY

☐ HIS REPLY ☐ HER REPLY

What would you consider the top 3 services in your life today?

☐ HER REPLY   ☐ HIS REPLY

☐ HIS REPLY   ☐ HER REPLY

Does time change from one day to the next and is this why some days seem to go on forever? Why?

☐ HER REPLY   ☐ HIS REPLY

☐ HIS REPLY   ☐ HER REPLY

How would you handle an individual with special needs that needed help?

☐ HER REPLY ☐ HIS REPLY ☐ HIS REPLY ☐ HER REPLY

Do you exercise? How has your exercising changed throughout your life?

☐ HER REPLY ☐ HIS REPLY ☐ HIS REPLY ☐ HER REPLY

What were the circumstances of your last relationship?

☐ HER REPLY   ☐ HIS REPLY   ☐ HIS REPLY   ☐ HER REPLY

What were the most difficult things you were told about your life growing up?

☐ HER REPLY   ☐ HIS REPLY   ☐ HIS REPLY   ☐ HER REPLY

Would you rather have them do it or have one do it for you?

☐ HER REPLY ☐ HIS REPLY

____

☐ HIS REPLY ☐ HER REPLY

____

If you could teach someone how to speak, would you and why?

☐ HER REPLY ☐ HIS REPLY

____

☐ HIS REPLY ☐ HER REPLY

____

What is one thing about it that you would have liked to have done differently?

☐ HER REPLY ☐ HIS REPLY

☐ HIS REPLY ☐ HER REPLY

What would you do if you were invisible for 24 hours?

☐ HER REPLY ☐ HIS REPLY

☐ HIS REPLY ☐ HER REPLY

What are your greatest achievements and what are your biggest disappointments?

☐ HER REPLY ☐ HIS REPLY   ☐ HIS REPLY ☐ HER REPLY

What's an average day like for you?

☐ HER REPLY ☐ HIS REPLY   ☐ HIS REPLY ☐ HER REPLY

How would you describe the feeling of the last two years?

☐ HER REPLY ☐ HIS REPLY

☐ HIS REPLY ☐ HER REPLY

Do you think humans will survive long enough to evolve into something different or will we make ourselves extinct before we have the chance to? Why?

☐ HER REPLY ☐ HIS REPLY

☐ HIS REPLY ☐ HER REPLY

Tell about a time when you had to face one of your greatest fears.

☐ HER REPLY ☐ HIS REPLY

☐ HIS REPLY ☐ HER REPLY

Which of the following people are most likely to affect your personal feelings?

☐ HER REPLY ☐ HIS REPLY

☐ HIS REPLY ☐ HER REPLY

What is the worst thing you've ever seen at a concert?

☐ HER REPLY ☐ HIS REPLY   ☐ HIS REPLY ☐ HER REPLY

If you had to choose one thing for that your mother would be proud of, what would it be?

☐ HER REPLY ☐ HIS REPLY   ☐ HIS REPLY ☐ HER REPLY

What's the best way you can approach a challenge?

☐ HER REPLY ☐ HIS REPLY   ☐ HIS REPLY ☐ HER REPLY

_______________________________   _______________________________
_______________________________   _______________________________
_______________________________   _______________________________
_______________________________   _______________________________
_______________________________   _______________________________
_______________________________   _______________________________
_______________________________   _______________________________
_______________________________   _______________________________

What did you get from this experience?

☐ HER REPLY ☐ HIS REPLY   ☐ HIS REPLY ☐ HER REPLY

_______________________________   _______________________________
_______________________________   _______________________________
_______________________________   _______________________________
_______________________________   _______________________________
_______________________________   _______________________________
_______________________________   _______________________________

What would happen if there were no cars, buses, trains, boats, or planes? How would this change your life?

☐ HER REPLY ☐ HIS REPLY

☐ HIS REPLY ☐ HER REPLY

How do you deal with an enemy that is so confident in their strength?

☐ HER REPLY ☐ HIS REPLY

☐ HIS REPLY ☐ HER REPLY

What do you want right now?

☐ HER REPLY ☐ HIS REPLY

____
____
____
____
____
____
____
____

☐ HIS REPLY ☐ HER REPLY

____
____
____
____
____
____
____
____

Where do you go when you want to be alone?

☐ HER REPLY ☐ HIS REPLY

____
____
____
____
____
____

☐ HIS REPLY ☐ HER REPLY

____
____
____
____
____
____

How do you find your place in life?

☐ HER REPLY   ☐ HIS REPLY

____

____

____

____

____

____

____

____

____

☐ HIS REPLY   ☐ HER REPLY

____

____

____

____

____

____

____

____

____

If you could be a person in the future who likes this person, how would that be?

☐ HER REPLY   ☐ HIS REPLY

____

____

____

____

____

____

____

____

☐ HIS REPLY   ☐ HER REPLY

____

____

____

____

____

____

____

____

What is the one thing that's the most important to you?

☐ HER REPLY ☐ HIS REPLY

☐ HIS REPLY ☐ HER REPLY

List of things that have served you so well over the years

☐ HER REPLY ☐ HIS REPLY

☐ HIS REPLY ☐ HER REPLY

What would you do if you knew you could get rid of a major problem
by having a huge number of people to whom you could give it?

□ HER REPLY   □ HIS REPLY   □ HIS REPLY   □ HER REPLY

How would you describe the feeling of being in the presence of
a seemingly unknowable person?

□ HER REPLY   □ HIS REPLY   □ HIS REPLY   □ HER REPLY

If you had to choose to have one accessory, what would it be and why?

☐ HER REPLY ☐ HIS REPLY

☐ HIS REPLY ☐ HER REPLY

Would you rather go back in time? Why?

☐ HER REPLY ☐ HIS REPLY

☐ HIS REPLY ☐ HER REPLY

If you could only take people with you on a trip around the world, who would you take and why?

☐ HER REPLY ☐ HIS REPLY

☐ HIS REPLY ☐ HER REPLY

What does "funny" mean to you?

☐ HER REPLY ☐ HIS REPLY

☐ HIS REPLY ☐ HER REPLY

Why do things have to stay as they are?

☐ HER REPLY ☐ HIS REPLY

____

☐ HIS REPLY ☐ HER REPLY

____

List of things that you found objectionable

☐ HER REPLY ☐ HIS REPLY

____

☐ HIS REPLY ☐ HER REPLY

____

Which body part would you choose to get a tattoo done?

☐ HER REPLY ☐ HIS REPLY

☐ HIS REPLY ☐ HER REPLY

What is the hardest thing you have ever done?

☐ HER REPLY ☐ HIS REPLY

☐ HIS REPLY ☐ HER REPLY

What is your father like in your daily life?

☐ HER REPLY ☐ HIS REPLY

☐ HIS REPLY ☐ HER REPLY

If you were given unlimited and unassailable power, what would you do with that power? Would you use it to help others, or would you use it to hurt them?

☐ HER REPLY ☐ HIS REPLY

☐ HIS REPLY ☐ HER REPLY

How do you know when you are ready to say goodbye to someone?

□ HER REPLY □ HIS REPLY

□ HIS REPLY □ HER REPLY

Do you have a fear of getting hurt? Why?

□ HER REPLY □ HIS REPLY

□ HIS REPLY □ HER REPLY

Name four items that can always be found in your refrigerator.

☐ HER REPLY ☐ HIS REPLY

☐ HIS REPLY ☐ HER REPLY

Would you rather not be able to read or not be able to write? Why?

☐ HER REPLY ☐ HIS REPLY

☐ HIS REPLY ☐ HER REPLY

If you had to choose one limb to survive, will it be right or left and why?

☐ HER REPLY ☐ HIS REPLY   ☐ HIS REPLY ☐ HER REPLY

Who is the most beautiful person you've ever seen?

☐ HER REPLY ☐ HIS REPLY   ☐ HIS REPLY ☐ HER REPLY

Do you do things out of the box? How?

☐ HER REPLY ☐ HIS REPLY

____

☐ HIS REPLY ☐ HER REPLY

____

What were you like in elementary?

☐ HER REPLY ☐ HIS REPLY

____

☐ HIS REPLY ☐ HER REPLY

____

If you can buy it in bulk, will you buy it?

☐ HER REPLY ☐ HIS REPLY

☐ HIS REPLY ☐ HER REPLY

What do you wish you were bold or brave enough to do?

☐ HER REPLY ☐ HIS REPLY

☐ HIS REPLY ☐ HER REPLY

How would you describe the feeling of not being able to do something you were supposed to do because of other factors?

☐ HER REPLY ☐ HIS REPLY

☐ HIS REPLY ☐ HER REPLY

List of things that you made up

☐ HER REPLY ☐ HIS REPLY

☐ HIS REPLY ☐ HER REPLY

Would you rather spend a week adrift at sea in a life raft or spend one month in the coldest place on earth? Why?

☐ HER REPLY ☐ HIS REPLY

☐ HIS REPLY ☐ HER REPLY

What is the one thing you think everybody does wrong?

☐ HER REPLY ☐ HIS REPLY

☐ HIS REPLY ☐ HER REPLY

If you had to choose one thing to change about today's society, what would it be?

☐ HER REPLY ☐ HIS REPLY

☐ HIS REPLY ☐ HER REPLY

How would you feel if you were going to be on TV?

☐ HER REPLY ☐ HIS REPLY

☐ HIS REPLY ☐ HER REPLY

If you could make one item disappear from your world, what would it be?

☐ HER REPLY ☐ HIS REPLY   ☐ HIS REPLY ☐ HER REPLY

What do you think about when you're by yourself?

☐ HER REPLY ☐ HIS REPLY   ☐ HIS REPLY ☐ HER REPLY

What is the best thing you learned from getting into music?

☐ HER REPLY ☐ HIS REPLY

☐ HIS REPLY ☐ HER REPLY

What do you think about when you get tired?

☐ HER REPLY ☐ HIS REPLY

☐ HIS REPLY ☐ HER REPLY

Why is exercise important to someone your age?

☐ HER REPLY ☐ HIS REPLY

☐ HIS REPLY ☐ HER REPLY

What is the one thing that you're most proud of with your group?

☐ HER REPLY ☐ HIS REPLY

☐ HIS REPLY ☐ HER REPLY

What is one thing you regret doing?

☐ HER REPLY ☐ HIS REPLY

☐ HIS REPLY ☐ HER REPLY

What do you do all day for fun?

☐ HER REPLY ☐ HIS REPLY

☐ HIS REPLY ☐ HER REPLY

What do you do when your heart is "filled with greed"?

☐ HER REPLY ☐ HIS REPLY

☐ HIS REPLY ☐ HER REPLY

What's your favorite thing about your city?

☐ HER REPLY ☐ HIS REPLY

☐ HIS REPLY ☐ HER REPLY

What do you do when you have an idea that you think is wrong and can't get out of your head?

☐ HER REPLY ☐ HIS REPLY

☐ HIS REPLY ☐ HER REPLY

How would you describe the feeling of being able to effectively use meditation in a daily life situation?

☐ HER REPLY ☐ HIS REPLY

☐ HIS REPLY ☐ HER REPLY

How do you deal with that kind of nonsense?

☐ HER REPLY ☐ HIS REPLY ☐ HIS REPLY ☐ HER REPLY

Explain what you would do if you won the lottery.

☐ HER REPLY ☐ HIS REPLY ☐ HIS REPLY ☐ HER REPLY

What would you like to do that hasn't been done?

☐ HER REPLY ☐ HIS REPLY ☐ HIS REPLY ☐ HER REPLY

How many projects do you have on your "to-do" list?

☐ HER REPLY ☐ HIS REPLY ☐ HIS REPLY ☐ HER REPLY

☐ HER REPLY ☐ HIS REPLY

☐ HIS REPLY ☐ HER REPLY

☐ HER REPLY ☐ HIS REPLY

☐ HIS REPLY ☐ HER REPLY

What do you believe makes you sad?

☐ HER REPLY ☐ HIS REPLY   ☐ HIS REPLY ☐ HER REPLY

How would you describe the feeling of being from a different culture?

☐ HER REPLY ☐ HIS REPLY   ☐ HIS REPLY ☐ HER REPLY

Would you rather spend your money on a real and personal connection to the people that have created the country you live in, or in spending your money and effort just to make a difference?

□ HER REPLY □ HIS REPLY

□ HIS REPLY □ HER REPLY

What is the one thing you will remember most of your life?

□ HER REPLY □ HIS REPLY

□ HIS REPLY □ HER REPLY

Do you have any worries that you're not getting lucky? Why?

☐ HER REPLY ☐ HIS REPLY

☐ HIS REPLY ☐ HER REPLY

Where's the place you hate?

☐ HER REPLY ☐ HIS REPLY

☐ HIS REPLY ☐ HER REPLY

What is your dream job?

☐ HER REPLY ☐ HIS REPLY

☐ HIS REPLY ☐ HER REPLY

What are you doing for yourself today?

☐ HER REPLY ☐ HIS REPLY

☐ HIS REPLY ☐ HER REPLY

How would you describe the feeling of indescribable despair like a kind of permanent sleep?

☐ HER REPLY ☐ HIS REPLY

☐ HIS REPLY ☐ HER REPLY

Would you rather fight a shark-filled river with a knife or a bow and arrow?

☐ HER REPLY ☐ HIS REPLY

☐ HIS REPLY ☐ HER REPLY

What's the best way to start a conversation?

☐ HER REPLY ☐ HIS REPLY

____

☐ HIS REPLY ☐ HER REPLY

____

What is most important to you to accomplish more?

☐ HER REPLY ☐ HIS REPLY

____

☐ HIS REPLY ☐ HER REPLY

____

If you had to choose one thing in life that you would want to do for the rest of your days, what would it be?

☐ HER REPLY ☐ HIS REPLY

☐ HIS REPLY ☐ HER REPLY

What's the single thing you've learned about yourself this year?

☐ HER REPLY ☐ HIS REPLY

☐ HIS REPLY ☐ HER REPLY

What would you do if you had a friend who was in trouble?

☐ HER REPLY ☐ HIS REPLY

☐ HIS REPLY ☐ HER REPLY

How should I motivate myself?

☐ HER REPLY ☐ HIS REPLY

☐ HIS REPLY ☐ HER REPLY

What is the one song that you wish you had written? Why did you choose it?

☐ HER REPLY ☐ HIS REPLY   ☐ HIS REPLY ☐ HER REPLY

You have one hour to come up with the most interesting television show, how can you describe and pitch it.

☐ HER REPLY ☐ HIS REPLY   ☐ HIS REPLY ☐ HER REPLY

Why do you think you've been doing so and so?

☐ HER REPLY ☐ HIS REPLY

☐ HIS REPLY ☐ HER REPLY

If you drew everything that came to your head, what would you be drawing right now?

☐ HER REPLY ☐ HIS REPLY

☐ HIS REPLY ☐ HER REPLY

Have you ever done anything in your life that was important enough for people to know about?

☐ HER REPLY ☐ HIS REPLY

☐ HIS REPLY ☐ HER REPLY

What is the most significant gain you have seen in the past five years?

☐ HER REPLY ☐ HIS REPLY

☐ HIS REPLY ☐ HER REPLY

Why do you need so many of them?

☐ HER REPLY ☐ HIS REPLY

☐ HIS REPLY ☐ HER REPLY

What is the one thing that you do that is unique to you?

☐ HER REPLY ☐ HIS REPLY

☐ HIS REPLY ☐ HER REPLY

Do you like driving your car? Why?

☐ HER REPLY ☐ HIS REPLY

☐ HIS REPLY ☐ HER REPLY

What did you want to be when you were a kid?

☐ HER REPLY ☐ HIS REPLY

☐ HIS REPLY ☐ HER REPLY

What song really makes you sad whenever you listen to it?

☐ HER REPLY ☐ HIS REPLY

☐ HIS REPLY ☐ HER REPLY

How do you see yourself in front of the mirror?

☐ HER REPLY ☐ HIS REPLY

☐ HIS REPLY ☐ HER REPLY

What does it mean to live a life of mystery?

☐ HER REPLY ☐ HIS REPLY

☐ HIS REPLY ☐ HER REPLY

Do you ever feel hopeless? Why?

☐ HER REPLY ☐ HIS REPLY

☐ HIS REPLY ☐ HER REPLY

Do you like working on your game?

☐ HER REPLY ☐ HIS REPLY

____

☐ HIS REPLY ☐ HER REPLY

____

What is most important to you when it comes to the future of the planet?

☐ HER REPLY ☐ HIS REPLY

____

☐ HIS REPLY ☐ HER REPLY

____

Was that a dream or something you expected to happen?

☐ HER REPLY ☐ HIS REPLY

☐ HIS REPLY ☐ HER REPLY

What are the top five things you wish?

☐ HER REPLY ☐ HIS REPLY

☐ HIS REPLY ☐ HER REPLY

What is the one piece of advice you want to give to someone who is considering taking on a career change?

☐ HER REPLY ☐ HIS REPLY

☐ HIS REPLY ☐ HER REPLY

How many people you've kissed?

☐ HER REPLY ☐ HIS REPLY

☐ HIS REPLY ☐ HER REPLY

What is your idea of perfect happiness?

☐ HER REPLY ☐ HIS REPLY

☐ HIS REPLY ☐ HER REPLY

Would you rather be a lion in the forest or a deer in the street?

☐ HER REPLY ☐ HIS REPLY

☐ HIS REPLY ☐ HER REPLY

Describe a time in your life when you lost control and tell why.

☐ HER REPLY ☐ HIS REPLY

☐ HIS REPLY ☐ HER REPLY

What is the most meaningful thing you've ever done by yourself in your life?

☐ HER REPLY ☐ HIS REPLY

☐ HIS REPLY ☐ HER REPLY

What made you the person you are right now?

☐ HER REPLY   ☐ HIS REPLY   ☐ HIS REPLY   ☐ HER REPLY

What animals are you most afraid of?

☐ HER REPLY   ☐ HIS REPLY   ☐ HIS REPLY   ☐ HER REPLY

How do you get rid of the stress?

□ HER REPLY   □ HIS REPLY

□ HIS REPLY   □ HER REPLY

Why do you act like you are?

□ HER REPLY   □ HIS REPLY

□ HIS REPLY   □ HER REPLY

What's your first reaction when you think about someone like your brother/sister?

☐ HER REPLY ☐ HIS REPLY

☐ HIS REPLY ☐ HER REPLY

What is one thing you would most prefer to improve in your life?

☐ HER REPLY ☐ HIS REPLY

☐ HIS REPLY ☐ HER REPLY

Which animal would most likely help you with your homework?

☐ HER REPLY ☐ HIS REPLY

☐ HIS REPLY ☐ HER REPLY

Do you have any tattoos? What do they mean? If you haven't, would you ever get some?

☐ HER REPLY ☐ HIS REPLY

☐ HIS REPLY ☐ HER REPLY

What is the most significant item for you?

☐ HER REPLY   ☐ HIS REPLY

☐ HIS REPLY   ☐ HER REPLY

Describe a time when you learned something important about your family history.

☐ HER REPLY   ☐ HIS REPLY

☐ HIS REPLY   ☐ HER REPLY

List of things that should be in your map but are not

☐ HER REPLY ☐ HIS REPLY

☐ HIS REPLY ☐ HER REPLY

What is the one thing that both of you value most in a relationship and can't live without?

☐ HER REPLY ☐ HIS REPLY

☐ HIS REPLY ☐ HER REPLY

What is one thing that makes you more likely to take action in an area where there is uncertainty?

☐ HER REPLY ☐ HIS REPLY   ☐ HIS REPLY ☐ HER REPLY

Tell about a time when you left the safety of a place or situation to explore or try something new.

☐ HER REPLY ☐ HIS REPLY   ☐ HIS REPLY ☐ HER REPLY

What seemed unusual on your morning commute today?

☐ HER REPLY ☐ HIS REPLY

☐ HIS REPLY ☐ HER REPLY

Where is your favorite place to live?

☐ HER REPLY ☐ HIS REPLY

☐ HIS REPLY ☐ HER REPLY

What would you prefer, a clean slate with fresh ideas or the old familiar and ultimately boring way of doing things?

☐ HER REPLY ☐ HIS REPLY   ☐ HIS REPLY ☐ HER REPLY

How do you deal with the fact that people will come and go?

☐ HER REPLY ☐ HIS REPLY   ☐ HIS REPLY ☐ HER REPLY

If you could give an amazing speech to the government, what would be the topic?

☐ HER REPLY   ☐ HIS REPLY   ☐ HIS REPLY   ☐ HER REPLY

How would you describe the feeling of being attacked by water?

☐ HER REPLY   ☐ HIS REPLY   ☐ HIS REPLY   ☐ HER REPLY

If you could be anybody, who would you be?

☐ HER REPLY ☐ HIS REPLY

☐ HIS REPLY ☐ HER REPLY

What is the one thing you would do to have the world change?

☐ HER REPLY ☐ HIS REPLY

☐ HIS REPLY ☐ HER REPLY

What is the biggest goal that you have for yourself at the moment?

☐ HER REPLY ☐ HIS REPLY

____
____
____
____
____
____
____
____

☐ HIS REPLY ☐ HER REPLY

____
____
____
____
____
____
____
____

How can you make a good impression on someone?

☐ HER REPLY ☐ HIS REPLY

____
____
____
____
____
____

☐ HIS REPLY ☐ HER REPLY

____
____
____
____
____
____

What would you do if you could work forever?

☐ HER REPLY ☐ HIS REPLY   ☐ HIS REPLY ☐ HER REPLY

How do you deal with a person who hates you so much that it drives you crazy?

☐ HER REPLY ☐ HIS REPLY   ☐ HIS REPLY ☐ HER REPLY

How do you deal with the aftermath of stress?

☐ HER REPLY ☐ HIS REPLY

☐ HIS REPLY ☐ HER REPLY

If you had to have one-on-one time with anyone, whom would you choose and why?

☐ HER REPLY ☐ HIS REPLY

☐ HIS REPLY ☐ HER REPLY

What color do you think your favorite color is?

☐ HER REPLY ☐ HIS REPLY

☐ HIS REPLY ☐ HER REPLY

When was the last time you watched one of your favorite shows that were actually good and not just on a nostalgic level?

☐ HER REPLY ☐ HIS REPLY

☐ HIS REPLY ☐ HER REPLY

If your life depended on one thing, what would it be?

☐ HER REPLY ☐ HIS REPLY

☐ HIS REPLY ☐ HER REPLY

Who are the people with whom you are willing to be friends?

☐ HER REPLY ☐ HIS REPLY

☐ HIS REPLY ☐ HER REPLY

What causes you to feel this way?

☐ HER REPLY ☐ HIS REPLY

____
____
____
____
____
____
____
____

☐ HIS REPLY ☐ HER REPLY

____
____
____
____
____
____
____
____

Would you rather be loved or feared?

☐ HER REPLY ☐ HIS REPLY

____
____
____
____
____
____
____

☐ HIS REPLY ☐ HER REPLY

____
____
____
____
____
____
____

What is the last thing you want the world to see?

☐ HER REPLY ☐ HIS REPLY

☐ HIS REPLY ☐ HER REPLY

If you could change one thing about the world today, what would it be?

☐ HER REPLY ☐ HIS REPLY

☐ HIS REPLY ☐ HER REPLY

If you had the power of fire, what would you do?

☐ HER REPLY ☐ HIS REPLY

☐ HIS REPLY ☐ HER REPLY

Tell about your favorite vacation experience.

☐ HER REPLY ☐ HIS REPLY

☐ HIS REPLY ☐ HER REPLY

What does it feel like to be happy?

☐ HER REPLY ☐ HIS REPLY

☐ HIS REPLY ☐ HER REPLY

What is your secret to life?

☐ HER REPLY ☐ HIS REPLY

☐ HIS REPLY ☐ HER REPLY

Would you rather get to know you and your personality? Why?

☐ HER REPLY ☐ HIS REPLY   ☐ HIS REPLY ☐ HER REPLY

If you could listen to any song that no one has ever heard before, what would it be?

☐ HER REPLY ☐ HIS REPLY   ☐ HIS REPLY ☐ HER REPLY

What's your first reaction when you learn a new language?

☐ HER REPLY ☐ HIS REPLY

☐ HIS REPLY ☐ HER REPLY

Do you prefer your own or others? Why?

☐ HER REPLY ☐ HIS REPLY

☐ HIS REPLY ☐ HER REPLY

What's the best memory you have from the last year?

☐ HER REPLY ☐ HIS REPLY

____
____
____
____
____
____
____
____

☐ HIS REPLY ☐ HER REPLY

____
____
____
____
____
____
____
____

What did you teach your daughter/son about being kind?

☐ HER REPLY ☐ HIS REPLY

____
____
____
____
____
____
____

☐ HIS REPLY ☐ HER REPLY

____
____
____
____
____
____
____

Did you figure out what's really happening? How?

☐ HER REPLY ☐ HIS REPLY

☐ HIS REPLY ☐ HER REPLY

What are your greatest ideas?

☐ HER REPLY ☐ HIS REPLY

☐ HIS REPLY ☐ HER REPLY

What is the most important thing that you have done in your life?

☐ HER REPLY ☐ HIS REPLY

☐ HIS REPLY ☐ HER REPLY

____
____
____
____
____
____
____
____

Why do you want so much?

☐ HER REPLY ☐ HIS REPLY

☐ HIS REPLY ☐ HER REPLY

____
____
____
____
____
____

Say something about your current health.

☐ HER REPLY ☐ HIS REPLY

☐ HIS REPLY ☐ HER REPLY

List of things that you want to do next

☐ HER REPLY ☐ HIS REPLY

☐ HIS REPLY ☐ HER REPLY

What's so horrible about the world that it isn't worth trying to fix?

☐ HER REPLY ☐ HIS REPLY   ☐ HIS REPLY ☐ HER REPLY

List of things that also got cut

☐ HER REPLY ☐ HIS REPLY   ☐ HIS REPLY ☐ HER REPLY